FIND THE HIDDEN INSECT

William Morrow & Company   New York 1979

FIND THE

HIDDEN INSECT

Joanna Cole & Jerome Wexler

Library of Congress Cataloging in Publication Data

Cole, Joanna.
    Find the hidden insect.

    Summary: Presents photographs of camouflaged insects accompanied by simple text explaining their behavior. The reader is asked to find the insect in each picture.
    1.   Insects–Behavior–Juvenile literature.
    2.   Camouflage (Biology)–Juvenile literature.
    [1.   Camouflage (Biology)   2.   Insects–Behavior]
    I.   Wexler, Jerome.   II.   Title.
    QL496.C64   595.7'05'7   79-18648
    ISBN 0-688-22203-X
    ISBN 0-688-32203-4 lib. bdg.

Design by Lynn Braswell

The author wishes to thank Dr. Randall T. Schuh, Assistant Curator, Entomology, of The American Museum of Natural History, for reading the manuscript.

Grateful acknowledgment is made for permission to use the following photographs: pages 14, 15, 34, 38 top, American Museum of Natural History; pages 35, 38 bottom, Animals Animals, © Walter Fendrich.

For Michael Oretsky

Can you see the insect in this picture? Of course you can. It is called a katydid, and it is looking right at you.

But not all insects are as easy to spot as this one.

Many insects need to stay hidden, because they have enemies like the hunting spider in the picture below. It lives mainly on insects, and so does the toad on the opposite page. These and other insect enemies–like birds, frogs, lizards, and even other insects themselves–use their sense of sight to help them capture their prey.

Like all animals that are hunted, insects have evolved ways of protecting themselves. Many insects have developed special ways of keeping hidden.

One of these ways is by appearing to be something else. There is an insect in this picture, but it looks like part of the tree. Can you believe that the lowest "twig" is really a caterpillar?

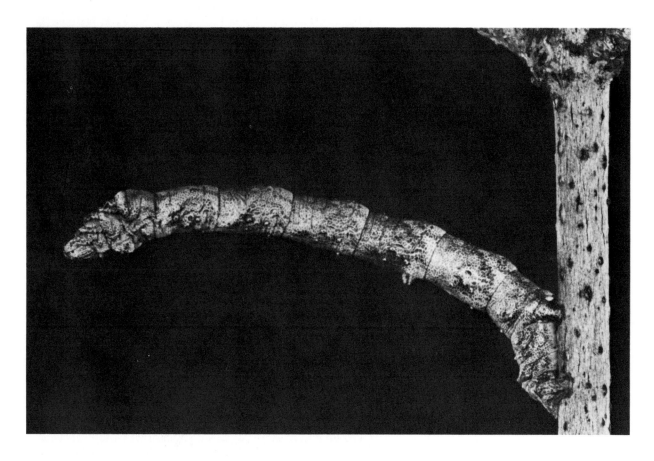

Up close you can see that the "twig" has legs and that they are holding onto the branch. This caterpillar of the inchworm family is a twig mimic. That is, it has the same shape, color, and texture as a twig. It even holds itself stiff like a twig.

Birds would eat this insect–*if* they could see what it really is.

Another common way of hiding is by blending in with the background. Caterpillars, which are soft-bodied and a favorite food of birds, often have this defense.

The caterpillar in the picture here is almost the same color as the leaf. Can you tell where the caterpillar ends and the leaf begins?

12

You can see it more easily
when it moves off the leaf.
Luckily for the caterpillar, it
lives on the leaves it eats, so
many enemies don't notice it.

13

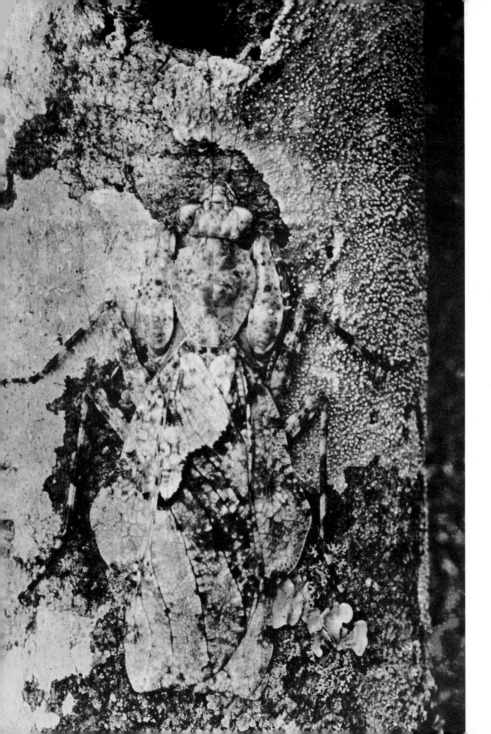

Some insects have markings that blend with their surroundings. Can you see the insect in this picture? It is a tropical praying mantis that blends in with the pattern of the bark of the tree.

Here is the same
picture, but an artist
has painted an outline
and shadows around
the insect. Only then
can we see it clearly.

This moth also rests on the bark of trees. Its markings help it blend with the bark. Even sharp-eyed birds often miss it. Did you?

16

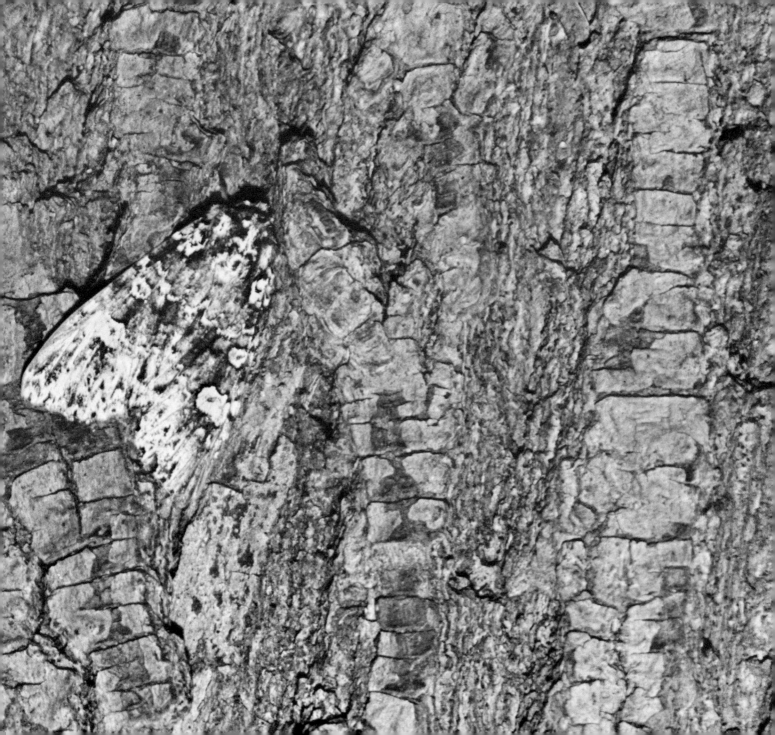

Another moth has color and markings that make it hard to see against certain flowers.

The syrphid fly is one insect that does not blend in with the background. It is easy to see, but its true nature is hidden in an unusual way. It is a wasp mimic.

Birds learn to stay away from wasps, because they taste bad and they sting. Because syrphid flies have bold stripes like wasps, birds stay away from them too.

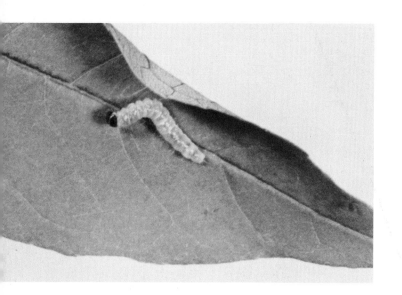

The caterpillar in this picture is not protected by color or mimicry. It is called a leaf roller, and it has another way of staying hidden. The leaf roller spins a thread of sticky silk. It pulls the edge of a leaf over and fastens it with the thread.

20

Now the insect is completely hidden and can eat in peace.

When it has chewed too many holes in the leaf, the caterpillar moves to another leaf and rolls it up too.

Some insects make hiding places with materials from their own body.

Hidden in the fuzz on this plant are many tiny insects. They are plant suckers called woolly aphids.

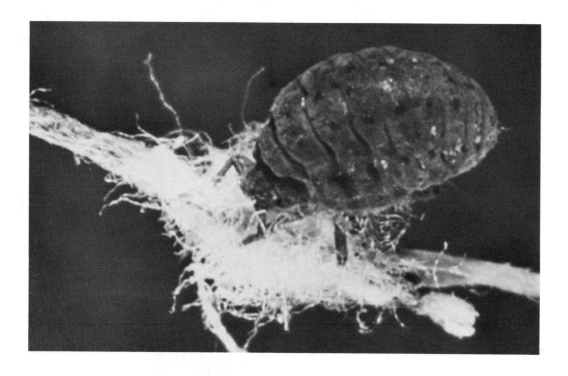

If someone pulls away the fuzz, you can see the aphid.

Other insects and birds eat aphids. But they cannot catch them easily under a layer of fuzz.

If a woolly aphid moves to another part of the plant, it must spin a new nest for itself.

Where is the insect
on this plant? It is hid-
den in the cluster of
bubbles. This insect is a
plant sucker called a
spittlebug, or a cuckoo-
spit bug.

The bubbles keep
the bug from drying out
and hide it from ene-
mies too.

24

If someone pokes it,
the spittlebug will
climb up the plant stem.

As soon as it finds a
new spot, the spittlebug
begins making a new
bubble nest.

In a short while, the spittlebug makes enough bubbles to cover itself up again.

One caterpillar of the inchworm family hides by covering itself with flower petals. This method works so well that it is almost impossible to find the caterpillar hidden in this Queen Anne's lace flower.

Even up close, you can barely see the insect.

Every few days the petals on its body die and turn brown. Then they no longer blend in with the rest of the flower.

The larva has to put on new petals. It pulls the old ones from its body with its mouth and lets them fall.

Then you can see that under the petals, the insect looks like an ordinary caterpillar.

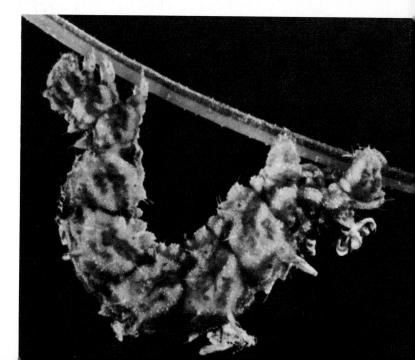

Now it begins
to put on its
flower "dress"
once more.
It plucks a petal
and attaches it to
its body with a
thread of silk
that it spins.
Soon the larva
will be safe again,
hidden from enemies
under its petal
cover. Eventually
it will spin a
cocoon and become
a moth.

33

Now you know a lot about how and where insects hide. Can you find the hidden insects on these pages? Information about each one is given on page 38-39.

34

35

36

Information about the insects shown on pages 34-37:

a. One of the "sticks" in the picture is a stick-mimicking insect called a walking stick. It is a relative of the grasshopper.

b. This strange-looking mantis comes from Turkey. Its body resembles growing plant stems.

c. The topmost "leaf" in the picture is actually a plant-sucking insect called a tree hopper.

d. There are two insects in this picture. The bee, which is easy to see, has been trapped by an ambush bug, which looks like part of the flower. When bees or butterflies visit the flower, the ambush bug captures them with its strong front legs and sharp beak.

Born in Newark, New Jersey, Joanna Cole grew up in East Orange. After attending the University of Massachusetts and Indiana University, she earned a B.A. degree in psychology at the City College of New York. Later she took graduate courses in elementary education at New York University and served for one year in a Brooklyn elementary school as a librarian. Mrs. Cole now is a children's book editor and lives in New York City with her husband and daughter.

Jerome Wexler was born in New York City, where he attended Pratt Institute. Later he studied at the University of Connecticut. His interest in photography started when he was in the ninth grade. After service in World War II, he worked for the State Department in Europe as a photographer. Returning to the United States, he specialized in photographing advanced farming techniques, and the pictures he made have been published throughout the world. Since then he has illustrated a number of children's books with his photographs of plants and animals.

At present, Mr. Wexler lives in Wallingford, Connecticut.